Contents

Words in **bold** can be found in the glossary on page 28

What is a village home?

A village is a small group of homes and other buildings. The buildings found in a village may include a church, a few small shops, a school or a village **hall**.

▼ *This is Godshill, a village on the Isle of Wight, England. The roofs are made of **thatch**.*

People who live in small villages often know each other. Meetings, activities and **festivals** take place in the village hall. Some villages are near big towns or cities, others can be far from anywhere.

▲ *The houses in this village in Sumatra have roofs made from* ***corrugated iron***.

Life in a village

People like village life because it is not as busy or crowded as life in a city. A lot of villages lie in beautiful **countryside**. Villages are smaller and they are often more peaceful than towns and cities.

▼ Over 1,000 people live in the beautiful village of Strafford in Vermont, USA.

Homes around the world

Village homes

Nicola Barber

First published in Great Britain in 2006 by Wayland,
an imprint of Hachette Children's Books

Copyright © 2006 Wayland

Hachette Children's Books
338 Euston Road, London NW1 3BH

Editor: Hayley Leach
Senior Design Manager: Rosamund Saunders
Designer: Elaine Wilkinson
Geography consultant: Ruth Jenkins

Printed and bound in China

British Library Cataloguing in Publication Data
Barber, Nicola
    Village home. - (Homes around the world)
    1.Dwellings - Juvenile literature 2.Country life - Juvenile
    literature 3.Villages - Juvenile literature
    I.Title
    643.1'091734

ISBN-10: 0-7502-4872-6
ISBN-13: 978-0-7502-4872-3

Cover photograph: the village of Roquebrune
in France.

Photo credits: nagelestock.com/Alamy 6, Peter
Horree/Alamy 7, Glen Allison/Getty 8, Lonely Planet
Images 9, Dennis Cox/Alamy 10, Sergio Pitamitz/Getty
11 and cover, Allison Wright/Corbis 12, Danita
Delimont/Alamy 13 and title page, Keren Su/China
Span/Alamy 14, Chris Lisle/Corbis 15,
GreekStockOne/Alamy 16, Dean Conger/Getty 17,
qaphotos.com/Alamy 18, Bruce Harber/Ecoscene 19,
Mark Boulton/Alamy 20, Lonely Planet Images 21, Peter
Bowater/Alamy 22, Janine Wiedel Photolibrary/Alamy
23, Jeff Morgan/Alamy 24, J Marshall – Tribaleye
Images/Alamy 25.

In some places, village life can be difficult. In poor villages, most people do not have much money. People may leave their villages to earn more money in the cities. They hope that life will be better there.

▲ *This family lives in a village near Quito in Ecuador, South America.*

Underground and hilltop homes

In some villages people use the land around them to build their homes. Cave homes can be made by digging down under the ground or by digging into cliffs.

Village life
About 40 million people live in cave homes in China today.

▲ You can see the doors and windows of these homes built into cliffs, in Shanxi province, China.

Villages may be built on hilltops or steep hillsides. The homes in this village are crowded on to the hilltop. The homes lie close together with narrow streets in-between.

▲ *The village of Roquebrune is in France.* **Tiles** *cover the roofs of the houses.*

Building a village home

People often use **materials** from nearby to build their village homes. Wood, stone, mud or even animal skins can be used for the walls. Palm leaves can be woven together to make the roof.

▼ *This house is in Peru. Wooden **stilts** raise it off the ground and keep it cool.*

The Masai people live in Kenya and Tanzania in Africa. To make their houses, the Masai stick poles into the ground. Then they **weave** a **frame** with thin branches around the poles. They cover the frame with cow dung and leave it to dry.

Village life
The smell of the dried dung helps to keep insects away from a Masai house.

▲ A woman fetches wood in a Masai village. It is the Masai women who usually build their houses.

Inside a village home

Around the world, people decorate the insides of their village homes in very different ways. This couple live in a village in Rajasthan, in northwest India. They have used a blue **dye**, called **indigo**, to decorate the walls of their home.

▼ *The blue dye on the walls of this house comes from the indigo plant grown in Rajasthan, India.*

This house is in the village of Zalipie in Poland. The women of the village paint their houses with beautiful flower patterns. Every year there is a competition to see who can paint the best decorations.

▲ *People come from all over Poland to see the decorated homes of Zalipie village.*

The weather

In villages where the weather is hot, people sometimes paint their houses white. Sunshine bounces off the white walls, keeping the inside of the house cool.

▼ These village homes are on the island of Mykonos, Greece.

In cold places, people try to keep their houses warm. Thick walls made from stone or wood help to keep houses warm even when it is cold and snowing outside.

▲ *Wood or coal fires help to keep homes warm in the winter in Artybash, Siberia.*

The environment

Villages may not have a supply of clean water. Every day, people walk from some villages to fetch water from far away. The water is needed for drinking and cooking, as well as washing.

▼ *Two women in South Africa fetch clean water. One pumps and the other collects the water.*

In an **ecovillage** people try to produce all the **energy** and food they need. A windmill can be used to make electricity. Animals such as sheep, goats and hens can be kept for milk and eggs.

Village life

In Africa, some women walk 16 kilometres every day to find clean water for their families.

▲ *These homes in Torup ecovillage in Denmark are made from* **recycled** *materials.*

School and play

Many villages have their own small schools which may only have a few pupils. Some villages do not have a school at all. Children may have to travel to the nearest town or city to go to school.

▼ In this school in Boravali, India, the children sit on the floor to do their work.

Children in a village often go to school together and play together. Many villages have playgrounds where children run around and have fun.

▲ Children play a ball game in their village in Laos.

Going to work

Many people live in a village and travel to the nearest town or city to go to work. They may have to travel a long way every day. Other people can do their work at home, using a computer.

▼ This man runs his business from home in a village in France. He can go to work in his garden!

Farmers often live in villages. They grow food for their families to eat. If they can, they also grow **crops** to sell at the **local** market. Some farmers keep animals, too.

▲ This farmer is picking mandarin fruit in Akyaka village in Turkey.

Getting about

Villages can be far away from the nearest town or city. Many do not have a railway line, and often there are few buses that go to the village. Cars are a popular way to get about.

▼ A bus picks up post from Llangwyryfon in Wales. It also takes people from village to village.

In some parts of the world, the roads between villages are very uneven and difficult to use. People walk or travel in carts to get about. They often use animals, such as camels or **mules**, to carry their goods.

Village life

In some villages, people share taxis and car journeys to help each other travel about.

▲ *In Myanmar cattle are used to pull carts.*

Where in the world?

Some of the places talked about in this book have been labelled here.

Look at the two different pictures on this map.

- How are the homes different from each other?

- What is each home made of?

- Look at their walls, roofs, windows and doors.

- How are these homes different from where you live?

- How are they the same?

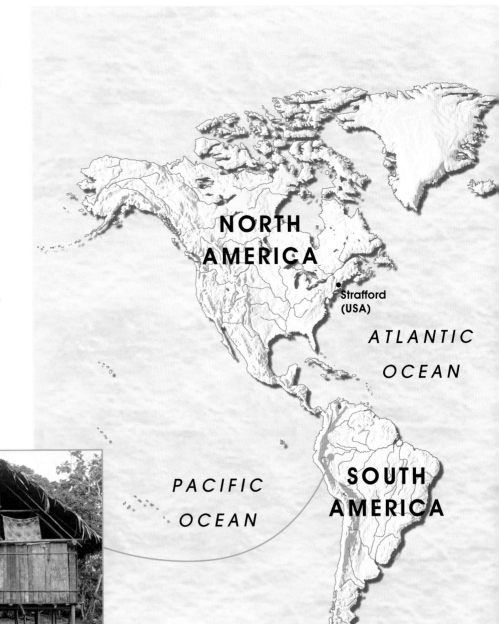

NORTH AMERICA

• Strafford (USA)

ATLANTIC OCEAN

PACIFIC OCEAN

SOUTH AMERICA

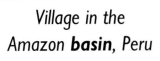

*Village in the Amazon **basin**, Peru*

N
W · E
S

ASIA

Torup
(DENMARK)

Llangwyryfon
(WALES)

EUROPE

Artybash
(RUSSIA)

shill
GLAND)

Zalipie
(POLAND)

Roquebrune
(FRANCE)

Akyaka
(TURKEY)

AFRICA

INDIA

SUMATRA

PACIFIC

OCEAN

AUSTRALASIA

ANTARCTICA

*Village on
the island
of Mykonos,
Greece*

Glossary

basin	the huge area drained by a river
corrugated iron	a sheet of iron that has ridges running along it
countryside	wide open spaces which are not in a town or city, such as fields or farmland
crop	plants grown for food or to sell
dye	a substance that gives colour to things
ecovillage	a village where people try to produce all their own energy, grow their own food, and be self-sufficient
energy	you need energy to make things work. Electricity is a kind of energy.
festival	a time of celebration
frame	a structure that gives something shape and strength
hall	a large room
indigo	a blue dye that comes from the indigo plant
local	near to home
material	what something is made from
mule	a cross between a donkey and a horse
recycled	describes an item that is made from something that has already been used and is no longer needed
stilts	poles that are used to raise something off the ground
tile	a thin slab made from hard material. Tiles are laid in rows to cover roofs, floors or walls.
thatch	a roof covering made from straw
weave	to thread in and out

Further information

Books to read

Starters Homes Rosie McCormick, Wayland (2003)

Going for a Walk: In the Village Sally Hewitt, Watts (2005)

A Year in the Village Sally Hewitt, Watts (2004)

We Come From India David Cumming, Wayland (1999)

We Come From China Julia Waterlow, Wayland (1999)

Websites

http://depts.washington.edu/chinaciv/home/3intrhme.htm#variation
About homes in China

http://indahnesia.com/indonesia/SUTHOU/batak_houses.php
About homes in Indonesia

http://archilibre.org/ENG/inspiration/zalipie.html
For more pictures of Zalipie

http://www.photo-gallery.dk/oversigt/lokaliteter/torup/preview_1of8.html
For more pictures of the Torup ecovillage

Index